Walking in the spring

by Beverley Randell

Spring days are longer than winter days. Some spring days are warm and sunny.

If you go for a walk in spring, you will see flowers. Some spring flowers are yellow, some are white, and some are blue.

You can see white **blossoms** on the apple trees.

You can see pink blossoms on the cherry trees.

Blossoms are flowers.

Some trees are starting
to get new green leaves.

If you go for a walk
by a farm in spring,
look for baby lambs.

Lambs run and jump,
and then they go back
to their mothers for a drink.

Down on the farm
you can see calves, too.

Sometimes you can see kids.
Kids are baby goats.

Farm dogs
have puppies.

Farm cats have kittens.

If you go for a walk
down by a river,
look for ducklings.
Little brown and yellow ducklings
will be swimming with their mothers.

Look for birds
with grass
in their beaks.
They are making nests.

Some birds
sing all day.
Summer
is coming.